OCCUPIED

OCCUPIED: A Field Guide to the Quiet Angst of Public Restrooms

James Perez

Occupied: A Field Guide to the Quiet Angst of Public Restrooms
Copyright © 2025 by James Perez

All rights reserved.
No part of this publication may be reproduced, stored in a retrieval system, or transmitted in any form or by any means—electronic, mechanical, photocopying, recording, or otherwise—without the prior written permission of the author, except in the case of brief quotations used in reviews, articles, or scholarly works.

Published by Private Moment Press

Cover design by James Perez / AI-assisted
Illustrations by James Perez / AI-assisted
Interior design by James Perez

ISBN: 979-8-9997255-0-9
Imprint: Private Moment Press

This is a work of creative nonfiction. Some names, places, and identifying details have been changed to protect the privacy of individuals. Any resemblance to real persons, living or dead, is purely coincidental.

First edition
Printed in the United States of America

10 9 8 7 6 5 4 3 2 1

Dedication

To my son–
may you always know when to laugh, when to flush, and when to hold your ground.

Table of Contents

Foreword

Dedication

Chapter 1: The Great Silence
Page 1

Chapter 2: The Fear of the Fart
Page 3

Chapter 3: Eye Contact Is Violence
Page 6

Chapter 4: Stalls: Our Solitary Sanctuaries
Page 9

Chapter 5: A Brief History of Bathroom Taboos
Page 12

Chapter 6: The Great Urinal Gap Debate
Page 15

Chapter 7: Hand-washing Theater
Page 18

Chapter 8: Whispering in the Water Closet
Page 21

Chapter 9: International Toilet Tourism
Page 24

Chapter 10: A Hopeful Flush
Page 27

Interlude: Inspiration in the Worst of Times
Page 29

Chapter 11: The Paper Throne
Page 31

Chapter 12: The Restroom Refuge
Page 34

Chapter 13: The Last Flush
Page 37

About the Author

Reader Reflection – Awkward Moments I've Witnessed in Public Bathrooms

Forward

Bathrooms. The great equalizer.
No matter who you are—CEO, barista, astronaut, or someone who still hasn't figured out how to use the motion-sensor sink—you've found yourself in the tiled theater of public restrooms, navigating the silent choreography of avoidance, timing, and dignity preservation.

Occupied by James Perez is not just a book about bathrooms. It's a book about us—about the strange, unspoken rules we follow to survive shared spaces without losing our minds (or our pride). With razor-sharp wit and a knack for turning the mundane into the meaningful, Perez takes us on a journey through the grout-lined corridors of human awkwardness, reminding us that even in our most vulnerable moments, we're all just trying to hold it together.

This is not a book for the pearl-clutchers. If you're the type to gasp at the mention of bodily functions, you might want to avert your eyes (and maybe your nose). But beneath the laughter, this book is a mirror—albeit one slightly smudged by soap and regret—reflecting the beautifully bizarre truth of human behavior.

Occupied is a laugh-out-loud field guide to the absurdity of public life, a love letter to the quiet heroes who flush with grace, and a gentle nudge to embrace the ridiculousness of being human.

So grab a copy, find a quiet corner (or stall), and prepare to see the world—and yourself—a little differently.

Just don't forget to wash your hands.

Chapter 1: The Great Silence

Chapter 1: The Great Silence

There's a moment—about three seconds after entering a public restroom—when something in the air changes. It's not the smell. It's not the lighting. It's **the sudden collapse of all human interaction.**

Voices drop off. Conversations die in mid-sentence. Laughter? Gone. You could walk into a restroom where two coworkers are cracking up about something just outside the door, and the second they step over the threshold, it's as if someone pressed *mute*. What follows is not peace. It's not serenity. It's a kind of polite panic—**a social power outage.**

I'm not new to this. I've been navigating this exact ritual my whole life. And to be clear: I'm not shy, I'm not timid, and I'm not particularly scandalized by the sounds of human bodies doing what human bodies do. But I've spent enough time in public bathrooms to know that this unspoken silence we all maintain isn't a coincidence. It's culture. It's collective etiquette. It's **the code.**

The rule is simple: **act like no one else exists.**

The bathroom is not a place for connection. It's a zone of neutralization. You drop your identity at the door. No small talk, no eye contact, no acknowledgment of the person two stalls over who just made a noise that defies the known laws of digestion. You don't flinch. You don't comment. You just breathe quietly and stare at the door like you're waiting for an elevator in hell.

It's not that we can't talk. We just **all silently agreed not to**. And I get it. There's something about being half-undressed, exposed to the echoes of porcelain acoustics, that makes even the most confident among us embrace discretion like it's a survival tactic.

I once shared a bathroom with a man who answered a call on his Bluetooth headset while at the urinal. Loudly. Assertively. With the same tone you'd use to close a deal in a boardroom, except the acoustics were giving the whole performance an accidental stadium reverb. "We're going to need to move that shipment before Thursday," he barked, as if urgency could drown out the very obvious trickle happening just below the phone.

To be clear, I wasn't offended. Honestly, I respected the efficiency. I just wondered how we got here—**to this moment where a man can juggle commerce and bladder relief with no loss of dignity.**

But that's the exception. Most of us uphold the code. The silence isn't about fear, and it's not really about privacy either. It's about mutual disinterest, which is a powerful form of kindness when you're at your most physically unceremonious. It's the closest thing we have to "don't ask, don't tell" for the digestive system.

And sure, I've waited a little longer before making noise in a stall. I've timed things to coincide with a toilet flush or a hand dryer kicking on. Not out of deep shame—just out of a **quiet respect for the ritual**. It's not about hiding. It's about knowing the game and choosing to play it.

The real beauty of the silence is that **it works.** It makes it possible for strangers to coexist in a tiled echo chamber without losing their collective minds. We don't talk. We don't look. We don't judge. And in that awkward, stifled, grout-lined stillness, we find a kind of temporary peace.

There's something almost poetic about it: a moment in our over-sharing, hyper-verbal, Tiktok-saturated lives where we all agree to just shut up for a second. To not perform. To not engage. To simply get in, do our business, and vanish.

We don't talk in the restroom—not because we're afraid to, but because it's the only place left where **we don't have to.**

And honestly? That's kind of beautiful.

Chapter 2: The Fear of the Fart

Chapter 2: The Fear of the Fart

We all say we don't care what people think. But then we find ourselves in a public restroom, cheeks clenched, knees slightly bent, hovering like we're trying to land a stealth aircraft—all because someone else is in the room, and **we absolutely refuse to be the one who breaks the sound barrier.**

Let's be honest. You've held one in. So have I. Not because we're ashamed of farting— we're adults, we understand how anatomy works—but because we know that in a public bathroom, **there's a difference between function and performance.** The fart is allowed. But not if it sounds too confident. Not if it draws attention. Not if it breaks the delicate acoustic truce of the space.

I've been in stalls where I could tell the guy next to me was waiting for a hand dryer to kick on so he could let one go. Not just waiting—**praying.** Like his dignity depended on 1,200 watts of manufactured white noise. That's the kind of calculus we do in here. Timing. Angles. Risk management. It's like launching a space probe except the payload is air and shame.

And look—I'm not judging. I've made those same calculations. I've sat in silence, listening like a predator in the jungle, waiting for just enough cover to drop my internal payload. I wasn't embarrassed. I was just **playing the game.** We all are.

Because here's the truth: it's not the fart itself that we're afraid of. It's the reaction. It's the possibility that someone in the next stall will recognize you, pause for half a beat, and think: Damn. It's not even criticism we fear—it's **being identified as the source of a specific sound.**

It's absurd. Every single person in a public restroom is there for some variation of the same purpose. And yet the moment that purpose becomes audible, we scramble to distance ourselves from it like someone just yelled "fire" on a plane.

Meanwhile, our coping strategies have become cultural artifacts. The courtesy flush. The fake cough. The synchronized hand dryer blast. One friend told me she calls it the **"sonic smokescreen"**—make some noise, mask your noise, pretend everything's fine.

Another friend—bold soul—told me he leans into it. "If it's gonna happen, I want it to be a power move," he said. "Announce your presence." This man, I should note, is either a fearless renegade or utterly unemployable in open-plan offices.

Women, from what I've gathered, have it even worse. Smaller restrooms. Shorter stalls. Greater expectations of grace. One woman told me she once ran the sink for **three full minutes** just to create a protective wall of white noise. "I wasn't washing anything," she said. "I was just holding space for dignity."

And that's really what this is all about. Dignity. Not the deep kind—the public kind. The image we construct of ourselves as clean, composed, odorless beings floating above the mess of humanity. The fart is a reminder that we're **very much of the flesh.**

It's not shameful. But it is inconvenient. And it punctures the illusion we've all built— that we're in control of ourselves. That we're the ones driving the machine, not just along for the ride.

So we wait. We mask. We contort. We try to release 12 PSI of compressed air in the quietest, most deniable way possible.

And when the inevitable happens—when the dryer fails, the timing's off, and the acoustics are not on your side—you own it. Or you pretend it wasn't you. Or, if you're like me, **you just accept it as part of the social contract we all signed somewhere around age seven.**

We fear the fart not because it's wrong—but because we know how much effort we're all putting into pretending we're not animals. And in that tiled chamber of denial, anything that pulls us back into reality sounds way too loud.

Chapter 3: Eye Contact Is Violence

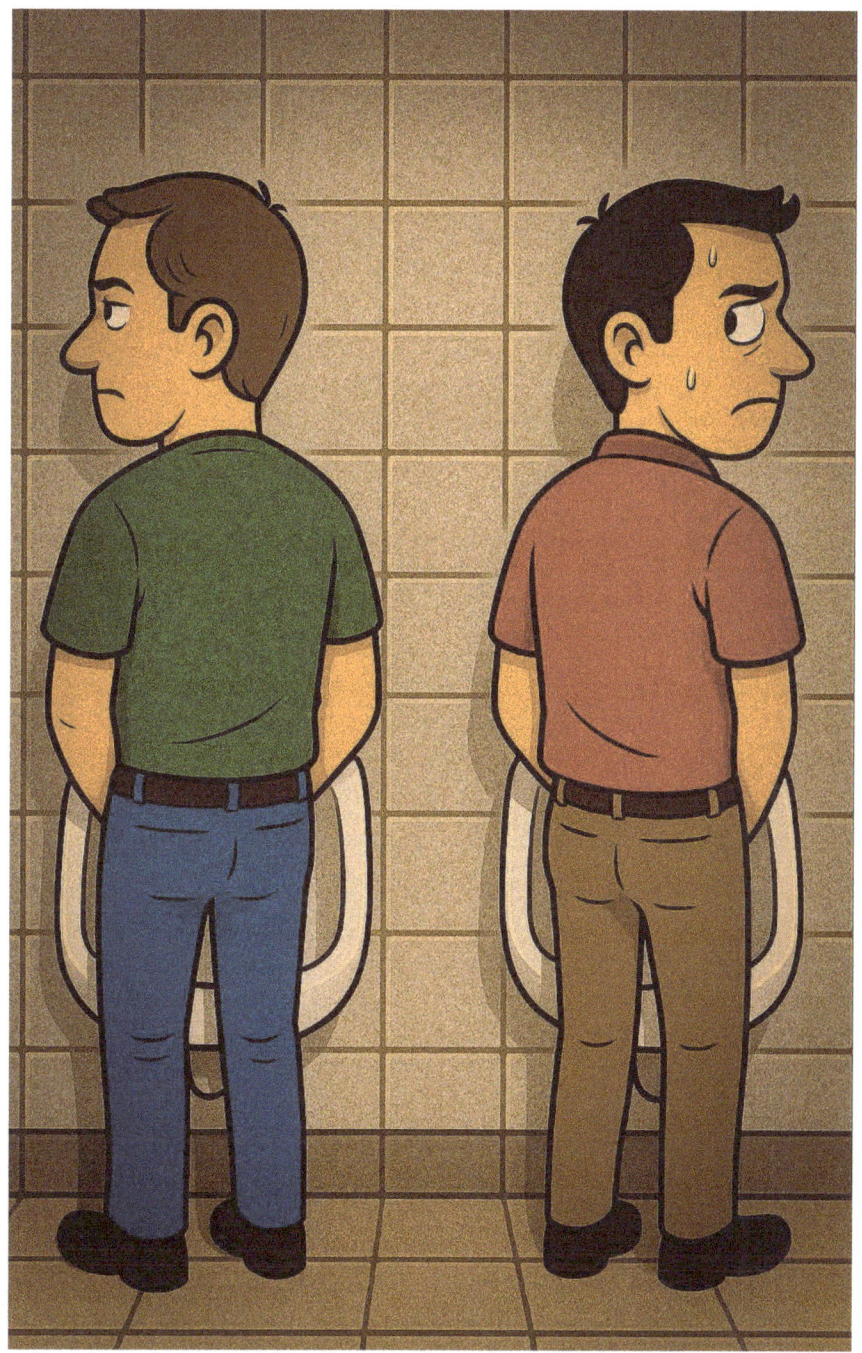

Chapter 3: Eye Contact Is Violence

The only thing that is more uncomfortable than making eye contact in a public restroom is making eye contact in a public restroom **while peeing**. It doesn't matter where—urinal, sink, mirror, hallway of shame on the way out— **eye contact in the bathroom is an act of psychological warfare.**

It's not that I'm afraid of people seeing me. It's that I'm afraid of them seeing me seeing them. We don't lock eyes in the restroom because it acknowledges the truth: *we're all pretending not to exist right now.*

At the urinal, the rules are ancient and precise. You look forward. Not left. Not right. Not down. Definitely not into the reflective tile across from you. **You pick a grout line and hold on for dear life.** If your eyes wander, even briefly, you've committed a social foul punishable by 30 seconds of chest-tightening silence.

I once caught a guy glancing sideways mid-stream. Just a flick. Not invasive. Not creepy. Probably accidental. And yet? **I have never fully recovered.** I think about that man sometimes when I'm trying to fall asleep. Not with anger. Not with fear. Just with the dull ache of having been seen in a place designed to make you invisible.

In the mirror, it's worse. There's something uniquely existential about washing your hands and accidentally catching someone's eye in the glass. You both know it's a mirror. You both know it was unintentional. But there's still a flash of panic—like you've been caught slipping out of a disguise. I once mouthed "I'm sorry" to a guy in a bathroom mirror because we made prolonged accidental eye contact. Not because I'd done anything wrong. Just because I felt something had been broken.

And if you must speak to someone in the bathroom, let it be after handwashing. When all parties are zipped, flushed, and reasonably composed. Even then, keep it brief. "Good game," if you're at a gym. "That guy in the stall is doing battle with something unholy," if you're bonding over a shared trauma. Otherwise? **No words. Only nods.**

What's wild is that this isn't taught. No one hands you a pamphlet at age thirteen labeled *Welcome to the Rules of Bathroom Disassociation.* We all just… *know.* It's absorbed, like shame through the air vents.

Even toddlers start picking it up. I've seen four-year-olds step into a public restroom, sense the mood shift, and go quiet like they just entered a sacred tomb. It's instinctive. A primal hush falls over us the moment we cross the threshold. **Do not speak. Do not look. Do not exist.**

And yet—and yet—we still try to socialize around bathrooms. There's always that one guy at the office who treats the restroom like his personal networking lounge. You're in there, just trying to survive, and suddenly he's like, "Hey man, you catch the game last night?"

Sir, I am **actively peeing**. This is not the time for sports talk. This is a quiet moment of personal reckoning. Read the room.

The bathroom, for all its tile and metal and harsh fluorescent lighting, is still **a room of human ritual**. And in that ritual, the avoidance of eye contact is more sacred than soap. It's not just etiquette—it's a form of mercy. We don't look at each other because to do so would be to **remind ourselves that we're all disgusting, fragile mammals trying to hold it together for another few hours.**

We're in this together. Silently. Invisibly. With great determination.

Eyes front. Grout line engaged.

Chapter 4: Stalls: Our Solitary Sanctuaries

Chapter 4: Stalls: Our Solitary Sanctuaries

The stall is a lie, and we all know it.

It's not private. It's not soundproof. It's not even fully enclosed. Most of them are basically three metal panels and a door that leaves a six-inch clearance on the bottom like it's been designed for dramatic prison breakouts. But despite all this, when we step into a stall, we act like we've been sealed into a sacred vault.

The psychology is fascinating. We've accepted this flimsy little booth as a kind of **temporary sanctuary**—a makeshift temple where we are free to be fully human without being perceived as such. Once the latch clicks shut, something in us relaxes. We're alone. Not actually, of course. We can still hear people breathing, shuffling, and unspooling way more toilet paper than seems reasonable. But somehow, that quarter-inch of warped metal paneling between us and the outside world becomes a force field. It grants us permission to exist without polish.

I've seen people do some of their **most honest thinking** in stalls. Big decisions. Tough texts. Existential scrolling. There's something about sitting pants down on a public toilet that clarifies your priorities. It's like being suspended between two worlds—one foot in the chaos outside, one foot in whatever's about to happen next. And in between: reflection, rumination, bowel movement.

It's not just the space. It's the moment. You can't rush a stall session. Even if you wanted to. You're in there for the duration of the event, and that enforced pause gives your brain time to file some overdue emotional paperwork. Ever noticed that some of your most unfiltered thoughts show up in the stall? That's not coincidence. That's **subconscious spring cleaning**.

Of course, the stall only feels private because we've all agreed to treat it that way. It's a group illusion, like airline applause or conference name tags. The truth is: we can hear each other. We know who's doing what. But we pretend we don't. That's the code. Someone could be fighting for their life in the next stall, and we'd just quietly wash our hands and give them space like a respectful ghost.

Chapter 4: Stalls: Our Solitary Sanctuaries

There's also a hierarchy of stalls. Everyone knows the end stall is for the shy and the anxious—it's the most private by geometry alone. The middle stall is a no-go zone. It's the Bermuda Triangle of bathroom placement. And the handicap stall—larger, roomier, often with its own ecosystems - is either a sacred haven or a guilt trip, depending on the urgency of your situation and how fast you can flush.

I once saw a guy exit the handicap stall looking like he'd just walked out of confession. He kept his head down, didn't meet anyone's eyes, practically sprinted to the sink like he

could wash off the sin. He didn't need to feel guilty. He just needed a little more space to do what the soul required. We've all been there.

What fascinates me most is how many of us use stalls as places to just **hide.** Not even to do anything. Just to be still. Regroup. Catch our breath. I've ducked into stalls during work parties, weddings, airport delays—moments when life got too loud and I needed the one place where no one would ask me a question. Not even the stall next to me.

And yes, it's a public toilet. Yes, the floor is weirdly sticky, and yes, you can see people's shoes shuffling in and out like they're auditioning for a tap dance number. But none of that matters. The stall is yours. For three minutes or fifteen, it's **your room in the world.**

It's not perfect. It's barely functional. But it's sacred.

And when someone tries the door and you have to hit them with the soft, ashamed "Occupied," it's not shame you feel. It's a small reminder: *you're in here, living your truth. And they'll just have to wait their turn.*

Chapter 5: A Brief History of Bathroom Taboos

Chapter 5: A Brief History of Bathroom Taboos

Public bathrooms in America are weird. Not just weird—weird **on purpose.** From the layout to the behavior to the absolute refusal to make eye contact, it all feels like something we inherited from people who really, really hated being reminded that they had bodies.

And you know what? We kind of did.

Let's start with the **Victorians**—the undisputed champions of polite repression. These were people who covered up piano legs because they found them *suggestive*. They invented an entire aesthetic around **never acknowledging the lower half of the body.** Unsurprisingly, they were also obsessed with plumbing, sanitation, and making sure no one ever spoke of what plumbing was *actually for*.

Bathrooms weren't called bathrooms. They were "powder rooms" or "water closets" or "lavatories"—a word that sounds vaguely French and safe, like you might be storing hand towels in there and not violently evacuating a burrito.

Fast forward to the 20th century, and we inherit this posture of politeness, now married to American **efficiency and paranoia.** Post-war modern design gave us the tiled, echoing, semi-private bathrooms we know today—engineered for cost, not comfort. Open bottoms, open tops, thin stall doors, motion sensors that go off like booby traps... all of it built to **move you along and discourage lingering**.

Privacy? Optional. Dignity? Up to you.

At the same time, we were busy sewing shame into the seams of society. Puritanical values stuck around like mildew: Don't talk about sex. Don't talk about bodies. Definitely don't talk about what those bodies are doing in the next stall. This gave rise to a cultural tension we still carry: bathrooms are both *necessary* and *unspeakable*. We all use them, but we act like they exist in a kind of dimensional rift—just out of sight, not quite real.

It's not just cultural, though—it's also political.

Take **racial segregation**. For much of American history, who was allowed to use which bathroom was a tool of oppression. Separate facilities were legally enforced, and even after desegregation, the public restroom remained a battleground of inclusion and exclusion. It still is.

Then there's the modern debate around gender-neutral restrooms, which you'd think would be a conversation about design or accessibility—but somehow it ends up being about everything *except* bathrooms. Identity, fear, discomfort, politics, projection. People aren't just arguing about plumbing—they're arguing about **who's allowed to be human in public.**

Chapter 5: A Brief History of Bathroom Taboos

And all the while, we've maintained this illusion that using the restroom is something to hide. Something we *all do* but must *never acknowledge*. Even in media, the bathroom is where the plot pauses. It's the one room where characters never have meaningful conversations unless it's a murder or a makeover. You rarely see a movie hero excusing themselves to go stress-poop before a big meeting. And yet—we know they must have.

Instead, we get sitcom gags. Fart jokes. Embarrassed exits. Nothing that actually explores the strange, quiet **rules we follow to protect ourselves from being too real in front of each other.**

But why?

Because bathrooms remind us we're not just personalities and opinions— we're walking meat tubes full of coffee and cortisol. They remind us that control is an illusion, dignity is contextual, and nobody escapes the universal truth: **eventually, you will have to go.**

So we cloak it. We build stalls that are thin enough to hear through but not see through. We create air fresheners that just add a floral layer of dishonesty. We invent phrases like "freshen up," as if we're all just ducks misting our faces before brunch.

What we avoid says just as much about us as what we obsess over. And in America, we've avoided bathrooms so effectively that we've made them into sacred awkward zones—**chambers of denial**, tiled and humming with polite fear.

Other cultures don't always share this approach. In Japan, toilets play music to **protect your dignity**. In parts of Europe, bathroom behavior is just... behavior. Not a secret. Not a shame. Just a thing you do and then move on.

But here? We treat it like a confessional booth you escape from as fast as possible— **hopefully unseen, and unjudged.**

And maybe that's the heart of it. The bathroom isn't just where we go to relieve ourselves. It's where we go to hide the parts of being human that we still haven't figured out how to accept. And until we do, we'll keep whispering "Occupied" like it's a password to a better version of ourselves.

Chapter 6: The Great URINAL GAP DEBATE

Chapter 6: The Great Urinal Gap Debate

You walk into a public restroom. Three urinals. One guy is at the far left.

You do not go to the middle.

You **do not** go to the middle.

You go far right. Because you are **a man of culture**, and you respect the most sacred of male bathroom laws: **leave a buffer**.

There are few things as universally understood and utterly unspoken as urinal spacing. There's no sign. No training video. No handbook. But every guy over the age of 12 knows the deal. If there are three urinals and one is taken, you take the furthest option. If the middle one is your only choice, you either wait, or—if the situation is urgent—you suffer the shame of breaking formation.

This is not about modesty. Nobody's looking. Nobody wants to look. It's about **proximity anxiety**—the primal discomfort of standing too close to another vulnerable man while doing something inherently undignified.

We don't talk about it. We just act on it, like birds migrating or dogs turning in circles before they lie down. It's instinctual. A survival mechanism passed down from urinal to urinal.

And when someone *does* violate the code—when they waltz into a five-urinal lineup and choose the one directly next to you—you notice. You don't say anything, of course. But something shifts inside. A small, subtle tightening of the soul. Not fear. Not anger. Just... **disruption**. The natural order has been disturbed. The sacred geometry broken. You stare forward and do your best not to sigh audibly.

There are, of course, exceptions.

Sporting events. Stadiums. Dive bars at 1:00 AM. In these places, all bets are off. The rules bend to accommodate volume, urgency, and poor lighting. But even then, you can sense the hesitation. The little internal wince as two men stand shoulder-to-shoulder, trying to pretend the situation is normal while pretending they aren't pretending it's normal.

And the eye contact? No. No, sir. We've covered that. Urinals are where eye contact goes to die. Your gaze stays locked forward like you're awaiting orders from Command. Some men look up at the wall. Some look straight down. Some just fixate on the manufacturer logo of the urinal itself, as if "American Standard" is delivering them quietly through the moment.

Chapter 6: The Great Urinal Gap Debate

The more stalls in a row, the more complex the math becomes. In a five-urinal setup, the optimal pattern is always: ends first, then skip one. If three men use urinals 1, 3, and 5, it's perfection. A symphony of spacing. Four men? That's when we start entering **high-stakes decision-making.**

Do you fill in next to someone? Do you pretend to check your phone while you wait for a gap to open up, even though you're clearly just scrolling nothing on an unlit lock screen? Do you abandon the urinal plan entirely and go for the stall like a rogue agent?

This is what's known as **tactical peeing**.

No one trains us in this. No one has to. It's just social gravity. And what makes it funny— what makes it worth writing about - is that it all comes from a place of **mutual respect**. We don't want to be looked at, judged, or chatted to midstream. And we assume you don't either. So, we all hold our breath and pretend to be very, very interested in whatever wall tile we're facing.

It's not about fear. It's not about shame. It's about not interfering with another man's brief moment of exposed vulnerability. We give each other space because we understand what this is: **a highly choreographed ritual of private relief in a public space.**

There's a kind of solidarity in it, really. A quiet, standoffish brotherhood forged over porcelain.

And if you forget the rules someday—if you bumble in and take the middle urinal unprovoked—no one will call you out. No one will curse you. But someone, somewhere in the room, will add your name to a list.

And they will never forget.

Chapter 7: Handwashing Theater

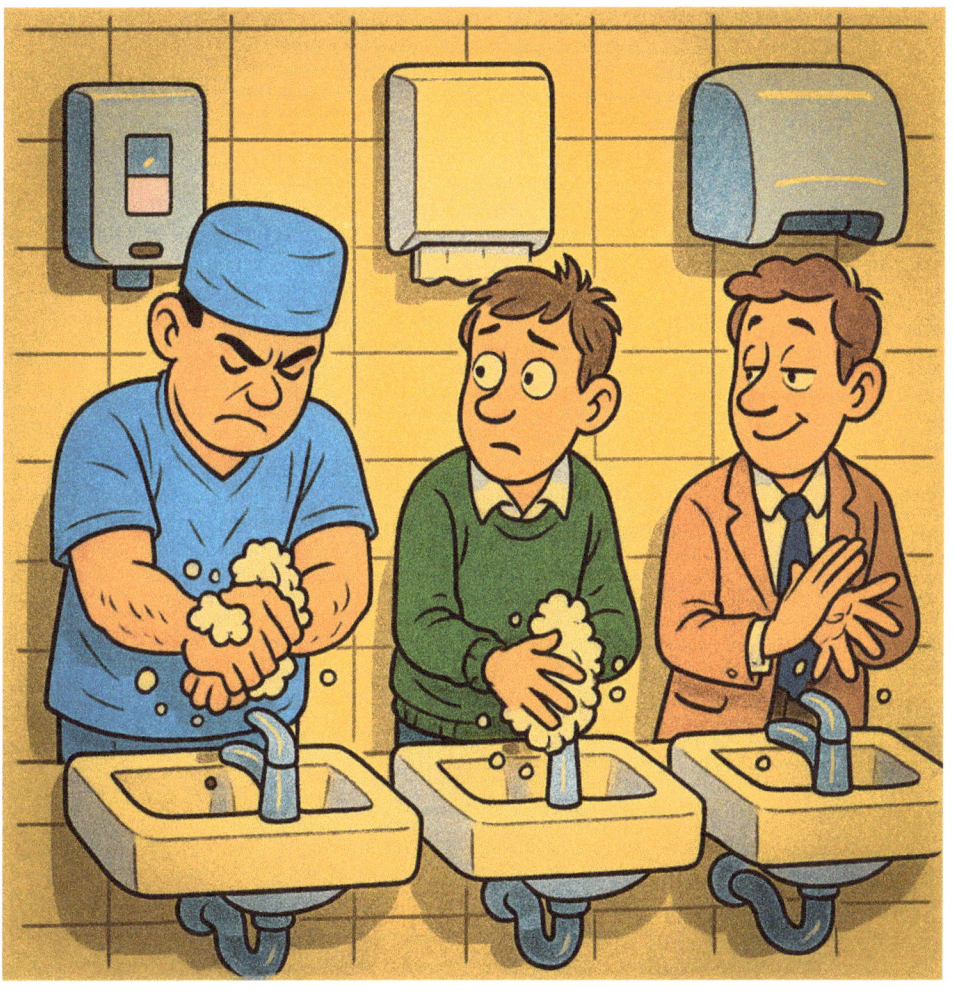

Chapter 7: Handwashing Theater

There's nothing like the eyes of a stranger watching you wash your hands to make you suddenly question **everything** about how you wash your hands.

Do I go for soap immediately? Am I lathering long enough? Was that rinse too short? Do I dry with paper towels? Air dryer? Pants? What if someone's watching the whole thing, mentally scoring my hygiene like it's a figure skating routine?

This is **handwashing theater** - a brief, silent performance we give for each other in public restrooms. It's part ritual, part social contract, and part guilt-driven improvisation. We're not just washing our hands. We're signaling: Look at me. I'm civilized. I'm trying.

We all know someone who doesn't wash their hands. Or we've at least seen them. You hear the flush, you hear the footsteps, and then the door swings open without so much as a pump of soap or a guilty splash of water. It's bold. Brazen. Borderline feral. You catch their reflection in the mirror as they walk out like **a man who's done this before and fears no consequence.**

The rest of us? We're doing what I call competitive cleanliness. The guy next to you soaps up, you soap up. He scrubs like a surgeon prepping for an organ transplant, suddenly you're scrubbing like you're about to deliver the organ. He rinses for ten seconds? You rinse for twelve. Someone walks in while you're halfway through? **You start over**. Can't have them thinking you're a half-washer.

It's not about health. It's about optics.

We want to be seen doing the thing we know we're supposed to do—even if no one's grading us. Even if it's 1:00 AM in a gas station bathroom and the only other guy in there is clearly just talking to the sink. Still. You lather like you're under inspection. You don't want to end up as someone else's "Can you believe that guy didn't wash his hands?" story.

And if you skip it? You feel it. Maybe not enough to go back in. But enough to hear a tiny voice whisper: *So this is who we are now.*

It's wild how performative it all is. Think about **how many people actually wash their hands at home the way they do in public?** Full 20-second scrub? Doubtful. Soap-to-elbow coverage? Unlikely. But out in the wild, we become these diligent, foam-slinging icons of modern hygiene. Because we're being seen. Because we don't want to be the *other guy*.

Chapter 7: Handwashing Theater

COVID cranked the performance up to eleven. Suddenly handwashing wasn't just a social cue, it was a civic duty. You couldn't even walk into a grocery store without a bottle of sanitizer appearing like a hotel concierge. People timed their handwashing like they were counting down to detonation. And the fear? Not of germs—**of being judged as someone who doesn't care.**

The sink area became a zone of moral clarity. Soap meant safety. Rinsing meant virtue. Air drying meant you were willing to wait for your halo. It was less about hand hygiene and more about signaling to the world: *I'm doing my part*. You weren't just washing your hands. You were **proving your humanity**.

But now? Now we're somewhere in between. Some people still wash like there's a global spotlight overhead. Others are clearly back to the two-second splash-and-dash, shaking off droplets like they're in a shampoo commercial for chaos.

Me? I try to stay consistent. I do the soap, the scrub, the rinse, the towel. Not because I'm being watched—but because I'm watching *myself*. I like the rhythm of it. The reset. And also, yes, because if I skip it, the shame clings to me like the ghost of Purell past.

Ultimately, handwashing in public isn't about cleanliness alone. It's about **being seen doing the right thing**, even when no one says a word. It's about acknowledging the social bond between strangers who agree: *This world is messy enough. Let's not make it worse with sticky hands and quiet betrayal.*

And so, we wash. For hygiene. For performance. For each other.

Now please—**dry responsibly.**

Chapter 8: Whispering in the Water Closet

21

Chapter 8: Whispering in the Water Closet

The public restroom is built on silence. It's our shared suspension of reality, the white-noise buffer zone where nobody asks questions and nobody answers them. So when someone **starts talking**—really talking—in that space, it's like a record scratch in a funeral home. Everyone freezes, and the energy in the room shifts from *let's all pretend we're alone* to *okay, what's happening here and how fast can I leave?*

This isn't small talk at the sink. This is **full-volume commentary from inside the stall.** Sometimes it's muttering. Sometimes it's a sigh that feels a little *too* personal. Sometimes, horrifyingly, it's a **phone call**.

Now look—I understand the temptation. You're in a stall. You've got a moment. Maybe you're behind on messages. Maybe your boss just texted, maybe your partner called. But the moment you answer the phone while your pants are around your ankles in a reverberating porcelain chamber? You've entered a different social realm. You've crossed into a zone where everyone around you has to participate in your decision.

One time, I heard a guy in the stall next to me accept a call from what sounded like a *job interview*. He lowered his voice slightly, but not enough to disguise the fact that he was doing a full "walk me through your experience" while surrounded by echoes of hand dryers and digestive disarray. I didn't feel secondhand embarrassment. I felt **awe**. I've seen less composure at weddings.

The best part? He never acknowledged where he was. Not a single "Hey, I'm in a weird spot right now" or "Can I call you back?" He just powered through, like he was sitting in a wood-paneled office and not a semi-public echo chamber with a toilet paper dispenser squeaking every twenty seconds.

That's what fascinates me: the **casual violation of the code**. Because to speak in a public restroom—especially from the stall—is to ignore every single rule we've all silently agreed to. No matter how introverted or socially anxious or emotionally fragile we are, **we still know not to talk in there.** That knowledge is built into us like a firmware update. And yet, every so often, someone hits the override button.

And sometimes, it's not even a phone call. It's just... *talking*. Commentary. Narration. Once I heard a guy drop a single "whoa" during his own bathroom moment. Not to someone else. Just... to himself. Out loud. That was it. One syllable, delivered with quiet gravity, like he had seen the face of God in a Chipotle aftermath.

Moments like that stay with you.

Chapter 8: Whispering in the Water Closet

But what's interesting is that we don't confront these people. We don't tell them to be quiet. We just get real still and real quiet ourselves, like scared wildlife sensing an unfamiliar noise. It's as if the social contract is so delicate that once it's broken, **we can only protect it by pretending it didn't happen.**

It's the same reason we freeze when someone laughs in a stall. Laughter is supposed to be the language of comfort, but in a public restroom, it sounds like **someone's losing control**, and nobody wants to be near that kind of raw honesty.

There are levels to this violation. Phone calls are the most egregious. Casual stall conversation with a coworker? That's a close second. Then there's bathroom humor *in the bathroom*, which is somehow even more uncomfortable than the act itself. Jokes are fine. But in the stall, jokes feel like *breaking the fourth wall of your own bodily function*.

That said, I'm not offended by these violations. I'm interested in them. Because I think the talkers—the whisperers, the gigglers, the "hey babe, I'm just in the bathroom, what's up?" crowd—are telling us something: **not everyone feels the same pressure to disappear while doing something human.**

Some people don't care. Some people want to multitask. Some people—God help them— are just comfortable being known.

And maybe, just maybe, they're right.

But if I'm honest? If I'm in the stall next to you, trying to mind my business, and I hear you accept a call with a chipper "Hey, what's up?"—my only thought is: *Sir, what's up is your echo is now my problem, and I just need a moment of peace in this vulnerable little box of lies.*

Because in the great theater of the restroom, **silence isn't just etiquette—it's kindness.** And some of us still believe in putting on a good show.

Chapter 9: International Toilet Tourism

Chapter 9: International Toilet Tourism

One of the fastest ways to realize how culturally specific bathroom behavior is? **Leave the country**.

Suddenly, all your instincts—stall strategies, silence rules, urinal etiquette—become irrelevant. You walk into a restroom abroad and you might as well be a confused raccoon in a power station. Nothing makes sense, but everything still works.

Let's start with **Japan**, a country where toilet design has advanced so far beyond American plumbing that it feels like you're peeing in the future. Japanese public restrooms often come equipped with a full control panel: bidet options, seat warming, sound-masking buttons, and sometimes even **music to hide your shame**. It's a complete rejection of awkward silence—not because they want noise, but because they **understand what the silence exposes.** So instead of pretending nothing's happening, they gently smother the moment in chimes and artificial waterfalls. It's thoughtful. It's hygienic. It's emotionally intelligent plumbing.

In Japan, *you're not weird for needing privacy*. The toilet helps you create it. That's **design as empathy**. Meanwhile, in the U.S., we build stalls that look like they were designed by someone who has never once pooped in public.

Then there's **Germany**, where the toilets sometimes feature what's known as a "**shelf toilet**." If you've never encountered this, I'll be delicate: rather than dropping into water immediately, your business lands on a small dry platform for... inspection. It's meant for checking your health, technically. But what it really creates is an incredibly confrontational experience. There is **no pretending you didn't just do that**. You see it. It sees you. And then you flush like you're trying to erase a crime.

American travelers who encounter shelf toilets often describe them with phrases like "deeply upsetting" or "emotionally loud." But Germans? They're practical about it. It's just biology. You look, you learn, you move on. It's not shameful—it's information.

In **France**, restrooms sometimes go full co-ed. You might walk into a bathroom labeled "Toilettes" and find a row of urinals on one side, and women touching up their makeup on the other, completely unbothered. And if you're from the U.S., your brain starts sending off alarm bells, because the invisible boundaries you're used to don't exist there. But no one else flinches. Because in France, **bodies aren't inherently scandalous**. They just are.

Chapter 9: International Toilet Tourism

In parts of **India**, you'll encounter squat toilets—no seat, just a platform and two foot placements. For the unprepared tourist, this can feel like being asked to do yoga under pressure. But again, there's logic to it. It's closer to how the body is designed to, well, *evacuate*. It's not primitive. It's functional. It's also a reminder that America's obsession with comfort sometimes makes us less adaptable than we like to believe.

In **Scandinavian countries**, public restrooms are often clean, modern, gender-neutral, and relatively quiet. No panic, no excessive rules, no weird codes of silence. Just **basic trust** that everyone knows how to behave like an adult.

What you start to realize is that **American bathroom culture isn't just about plumbing**—it's about **control, shame, and denial.** We're taught to pretend our bodies are silent, odorless machines, and anything less is a moral failure. That's why we build half-stalls with gaping floor gaps. That's why we layer every sound in apology. That's why we look at international restrooms not with curiosity, but with suspicion.

It's not that other cultures don't care about cleanliness or privacy. It's that they don't weaponize **awkwardness** the way we do.

They see the bathroom as a tool. We see it as a test.

And honestly? After standing in a Japanese toilet stall listening to bird song and feeling the subtle warmth of a heated seat, I started to wonder if we'd taken a wrong turn somewhere. If maybe—just maybe—we'd built a bathroom culture not to support our humanity but to **hide it.**

Maybe it's time to look abroad, not just for design upgrades, but for a healthier relationship with the fact that **we're all just here to take care of business.**

No shame. No drama. Just a little dignity, and maybe some polite music to ease us through.

Chapter 10:

Chapter 10: A Hopeful Flush

It's easy to laugh at public bathrooms. They're absurd. They're awkward. They're noisy and quiet in all the wrong ways. You're often surrounded by strangers yet desperately trying to pretend you're alone. You're at your most human, and somehow also your most invisible.

And yet—**they're everywhere**. Restrooms are some of the most universal spaces we share. Doesn't matter whether your race, gender, class, or Wi-Fi password—eventually, your body will remind you that you're not above biology, and when it does, you'll be making your way to a tiled room with a broken soap dispenser and a sink that requires interpretive dance to activate.

So maybe it's time we stop pretending this is all some personal failure and start calling it what it is: **a shared experience**, one that deserves a little more honesty, a little less shame, and maybe a soft chuckle along the way.

Yes, we play strange games in restrooms. We coordinate coughs with gas. We perform handwashing like we're up for review. We act like silence is sacred and eye contact is a sin. But all that effort—that entire ballet of avoidance—is just a way of saying, *"I know you're human. And I'm trying not to make it harder for you to be one."*

That's kind of beautiful, isn't it?

And sure, some people will keep answering phone calls in stalls. Some will skip the soap. Some will talk to you while your mid-stream like it's a team-building exercise. There's no fixing everyone.

But if this book has done anything—beyond keeping you company while you handle your business—I hope it gives you permission to laugh at the whole thing. To **see the absurdity without feeling embarrassed by it.** To know that we're all in this together, even if we're not making eye contact while we're doing it.

And maybe next time you're in a stall, or waiting for the only dryer that works, or deciding how long to hover before flushing something you'd rather not acknowledge— you'll smile. Not out of pride, but out of understanding.

Because this isn't just a bathroom. It's a tiny, tiled monument to our shared ridiculousness. And I, for one, think we've earned the right to laugh before we flush.

Interlude: Inspiration in the Worst of Times

Interlude: Inspiration in the Worst of Times

Psst...Let me tell you a little story.

The chapters you've read so far? They were written in moments of clarity, humor, and the occasional awkward memory. But the chapters ahead? They came from a slightly different place—a place of *intestinal reflection* and *questionable lunch choices*.

It was a Tuesday. A long, uncomfortable Tuesday. The kind of day where your stomach decides to send you a **strongly worded memo** about your dietary decisions. I won't name names, but let's just say the culprit rhymed with "*sketchy burrito.*"

I was at work, trying to hold it together, when the first rumble hit. You know the one. The *warning shot*. The *"you should probably find a bathroom soon"* kind of rumble. I ignored it, of course. Rookie mistake. By the time the second rumble came, I was speed-walking down the hallway like my dignity depended on it—which, let's be honest, **it did.**

And there I was, in the stall, sweating, regretting every decision that had led me to this moment. But as I sat there, contemplating my life choices and staring at the back of the stall door, **something unexpected happened**. I started thinking about toilets. Not just the one I was currently occupying, but toilets in general. Their design. Their purpose. Their quiet, unassuming role in our lives.

It hit me: **I had missed something**. There was more to say. More to explore. Even in the most *uncomfortable* of times, the toilet could still inspire meaning of some sort.

So, I grabbed my phone (**don't judge me**) and started jotting down notes. Ideas. Observations. The kind of thoughts you only have when you're sitting in a stall, wondering if you'll ever feel normal again.

The chapters that follow aren't groundbreaking revelations. They're not going to change your life or make you rethink the universe. But they do dig a little deeper into the quirks of bathroom behavior—the rituals of toilet tissue, the strange psychology of stall lingering, and the quiet moments we spend in tiled solitude.

So **buckle up**, dear reader. The next few chapters might be a little more reflective, a little more tissue-centric, but they're still part of the same journey. Because if there's one thing I've learned, it's this: even when life feels like it's flushing you down the drain, there's still room for humor, observation, and maybe—just maybe—**a little inspiration.**

Chapter 11:

Chapter 11: The Paper Throne

There's a ritual that happens in public restrooms—silent, swift, oddly precise. A person walks into a stall, eyes the seat, and performs a quiet, frantic origami routine with toilet paper. Strip by strip, they create a makeshift throne. A barrier. A moat. A **declaration**: "Not today, *germs*."

It's not just about hygiene. It's **theater**. A subtle dance of self-preservation and paranoia. Some people lay down an even single layer, like they're prepping for surgery. Others go full fortress—quadruple-ply insulation with edges tucked for wind resistance. Then there are the rebels who hover, legs trembling, determined to remain airborne like it's a CrossFit challenge.

But here's the thing: the **paper throne** isn't just about bacteria. It's about *control*. In a space where everything feels exposed and nothing feels sacred, placing those strips of tissue is a small, tactile way to say, *"I'm in charge of this part."* It's a moment of agency in an otherwise chaotic, tiled universe.

And let's be honest: we're not protecting ourselves from disease. We're protecting ourselves from **ick**. From imagined shame. From that one moment when you sit down too quickly and something is... *moist*. That's when the soul leaves the body.

But the ritual doesn't stop there. Have you ever noticed the **variations** in throne-building techniques? There's the **minimalist**, who uses just enough paper to cover the essentials, like they're rationing for the apocalypse. Then there's the **perfectionist**, who smooths out every wrinkle and double-checks for gaps, as if the toilet seat is about to be graded. And finally, the **overachiever**, who layers so much paper that the seat looks like it's wearing a puffy winter coat.

The irony? Studies suggest you're more likely to get sick from the **doorknob** on your way out than the seat itself. But logic has no place here. This is about **dignity**. About drawing a line—literally—between you and whatever horror story your imagination tells you happened on that porcelain ring.

Chapter 11: The Paper Throne

And yet, the **paper throne** is not without its flaws. The slightest misstep—a gust of air from the stall door, a poorly placed strip—and the whole structure collapses. You're left scrambling, trying to rebuild your fortress while maintaining the illusion that you're calm, composed, and definitely not panicking.

But perhaps the most fascinating part of the **paper throne ritual** is its universality. It transcends borders, languages, and cultures. Whether you're in a gas station in Kansas or a café in Paris, you'll find someone meticulously layering toilet paper like they're preparing for a royal coronation. It's a shared human experience, a quiet acknowledgment that, deep down, we're all just trying to make it through the day without sitting in someone else's mistakes.

And let's not forget the **hoverers**—those brave souls who reject the throne entirely. They squat, legs trembling, core engaged, determined to remain airborne like they're auditioning for a fitness commercial. It's a bold move, but one that comes with its own risks. A slip, a wobble, and suddenly you're closer to the seat than you ever intended.

In the end, the paper throne is more than just a barrier. It's a symbol. A tiny act of rebellion against the chaos of the world. And when someone tries the door and you have to whisper "*Occupied*" while clinging to your tissue tower like a squirrel in a thunderstorm, it's not shame you feel. It's pride. Because in that moment, you've claimed your space. You've built your fortress. And you've reminded yourself that, even in the most awkward of places, you're still the ruler of your own tiny, tiled kingdom.

Chapter 12:

Chapter 12: The Restroom Refuge

We've all heard the complaint: *"Why are you in there so long?"*

It's not always about digestion. Sometimes, it's about **escape**.

For men, the public restroom is often the last place on Earth where **nobody expects anything**. No **emails**, no **small talk**, no **decision-making**. Just tile, stillness, and maybe the sound of someone humming while pretending not to exist.

Some guys finish their business and linger. They scroll news, watch sports clips, play chess with bots. It's not **laziness**—it's **sanctuary**. The stall becomes a portal to **mental recalibration**. A seven-minute meditation chamber with questionable lighting.

But here's what might surprise some readers: **women do it too**. Differently, but just as intentionally.

Women's restrooms often double as **communal sanctuaries**. Spaces for **recalibrating emotions**, fixing smudged eyeliner, or escaping uncomfortable social energy. Sometimes, it's a chance to **breathe**, **text a friend**, or just **sit without expectations.**

A 2018 survey by the hygiene brand INITIAL found that **more than 1 in 3 women** admitted to using the restroom to **avoid social interaction**, decompress, or take a mental break. And while men might retreat into a stall for silence, women are more likely to have **full emotional check-ins** in front of a mirror or whispered between stalls like sacred confessions.

Still, the logic is the same: restrooms are one of the **few spaces** in public life where **being alone isn't suspicious**, and **lingering isn't judged**—as long as you flush eventually.

Even restroom design reflects this. Women's restrooms often have couches, longer counters, and more mirrors—not just for utility, but because society quietly acknowledges: **this is where women recharge**.

Chapter 12: The Restroom Refuge

Men, on the other hand, get cold tiles, cracked soap dispensers, and industrial lighting bright enough to trigger existential crises.

But regardless of gender, the restroom is a place of **unspoken amnesty**. No one asks why you're in there. No one questions what you're doing. You exist outside the realm of obligation— briefly, blessedly **off the grid**.

And yes, maybe we should all have better outlets for our stress. Healthier ways to reset than pretending to tie a shoe in a locked stall while scrolling Reddit. But until then?

The restroom remains our **reset button**. The one place where it's okay to take too long, to sigh too deeply, and to just… exist.

Chapter 13:

Chapter 13: The Last Flush

At some point, every visit ends.

The toilet flushes. The paper throne disintegrates. The hand dryer huffs its lukewarm breath. And you step back into the world, marginally lighter but somehow more **aware** of your **humanity**.

Bathrooms are not sacred spaces. They're not profound by design. But they are **profoundly human**.

They are where we strip off our layers—**literal and emotional**—and momentarily accept the parts of ourselves we spend all day pretending don't exist. They are where strangers gather in **silence** and manage not to lose their minds. They are the stage for some of our **weirdest rituals**, our **deepest discomforts**, and our **quietest victories**.

This book is not really about bathrooms. It's about us. The **weird, anxious, odor-fearing, overcompensating**, wildly **beautiful humans** trying to get through the day with dignity intact.

And if you've ever whispered **"occupied"** like it was your last line in a play—know this: you're not alone.

We're all in this together. **Stall by stall. Flush by flush.**

And if we can learn to **laugh** about it?

That's the real **relief**.

Flushed

About the Author

James Perez was born overseas to military parents, served in uniform himself, and now spends his time in unusually tidy places, bathrooms and mindsets included. He wrote "Occupied" as a field guide to the strange choreography of public bathrooms and the anxious, awkward humans trying to survive them. This is his debut book. He lives abroad yet still can't escape the scent of insecurity that lingers in every tiled corridor.

Public restrooms might be quick stops, but they carry the strange gravity of social theater. You step in, and without prompting, a whole set of unspoken behaviors unfold: the pause, the shuffle, the gaze-down silence. It's a performance that exists to avoid acknowledging that we're just... people, doing people things.

At its core, Occupied isn't just about bathrooms—it's about people. How we manage discomfort, protect our pride, and try to stay human in shared spaces. James has spent much of his life surrounded by individuals who don't always realize how brightly they shine in the shadows of daily life. This book is part observation, part quiet admiration—for those who carry awkwardness with grace and keep showing up anyway. This book is his quiet nod to them—and to all of us—stumbling through our shared humanity one flush at a time.

When not observing the strange ballet of public life, James can be found swapping stories with strangers, overthinking airport seating charts, or wondering why hand dryers still haven't figured it out.

Reader Reflection – Awkward Moments I've Witnessed in Public Bathrooms

No pressure. But we know you've seen some things.

1. _____

2. _____

3. _____

4. _____

5. _____

Feel free to keep going on a napkin, the stall wall, or just in your head. We've all been there.

We've all been there—those hilariously awkward, cringe-worthy, or downright bizarre moments in public restrooms that stick with us forever. Now it's your turn to share!

Use the hashtag #OccupiedMoments on social media to tell the world about your funniest, most awkward, or most relatable bathroom experiences.

Whether it's a stall mishap, a handwashing showdown, or a silent battle for the last paper towel, your story could inspire laughter, connection, and maybe even a little solidarity.

Here's how to join the fun:
Post Your Story: Share your bathroom tale on Instagram using #OccupiedMoments.

Tag the Author: Don't forget to tag me (@beatsjaime) so I can laugh along with you!

Spread the Word: Encourage your friends to share their stories too. The more, the merrier (and the funnier).

Let's turn the awkward into the awesome and build a community of readers who know how to laugh at life's tiled absurdities. Because if there's one thing we've learned from Occupied, it's this: we're all in this together—stall by stall, flush by flush.

So go ahead—share your #OccupiedMoments. I can't wait to read them!

www.ingramcontent.com/pod-product-compliance
Lightning Source LLC
Chambersburg PA
CBHW050817090426
42736CB00022B/3488